THE LAUGHING BABY

THE LAUGHING BABY

Remembering Nursery Rhymes and Reasons

Anne Scott

BERGIN & GARVEY PUBLISHERS
NEW YORK • WESTPORT, CONNECTICUT • LONDON

Library of Congress Cataloging-in-Publication Data

The laughing baby.

   Bibliography: p. 115
   Summary: A collection of nursery rhymes and play rhymes with
instructions for the accompanying finger plays or physical activities,
including clapping, bouncing, lifting, and tickling. Includes music for those
rhymes which are also songs.
   1. Finger play—Juvenile literature. 2. Nursery rhymes. 3. Children's
songs. [1. Finger play. 2. Nursery rhymes. 3. Songs] I. Scott, Anne
(Anne Leolani)
GV1218.F5L38 1987   793.4   87-13707
ISBN 0-89789-121-X (alk. paper)
ISBN 0-89789-122-8 (pbk. : alk. paper)

Copyright © 1987 by Bergin & Garvey Publishers, Inc.

Library of Congress Catalog Card Number: 87-13707
ISBN: 0-89789-121-X

First published in 1987

Bergin & Garvey Publishers, One Madison Avenue, New York, NY 10010
A division of Greenwood Press, Inc.

Printed in the United States of America

The paper used in this book complies with the
Permanent Paper Standard issued by the National
Information Standards Organization (Z39.48-1984).

10 9 8 7 6 5 4

Acknowledgments

"All for Baby" from *Finger Plays for Nursery and Kindergarten* by Emily
Poulsson, published by Dover, 1971.

"Baby Bye" from *The Baby's Lap Book* by Kate Chorao, published by
E.P. Dutton, 1977.

"Ballad of Downal Baun" from *Wild Earth and Other Poems* by Padraic
Colum, published by Macmillan, nd.

"Mix a Pancake" from *Sing-Song* by Christina G. Rossetti, published
by Macmillan, 1924.

"The Sleepy Song" from *Poems* by Josephine Daskam Bacon, published by Charles Scribner's Sons, 1903.

"Windsong" and "Lullaby" from *The Indians' Book* by Natalie Curtis,
published by Harper & Row, 1950. By permission of Barbara B.
Wedell.

Illustrations by Lura Schwarz Smith

Musical score calligraphy by Donna Dee Politi

To Zoë and Maya, the reasons that this book exists, and to Steve, who challenged and encouraged me to write this book. Also to my mother, who has spent many hours bouncing my babies on her knees so that I could write.

With special thanks to the mothers, grandmothers, fathers, and grandfathers who gave me their songs. They wrote to their homelands and brought me songs that have been passed down for many years. I also especially thank Irma (Colombia), Josephine (Ivory Coast), Joyce and Kozo (Japan), Mieko (Japan), Marina (Soviet Union), Madame de Gery (France), Rosemary (Panama), Kam Lin (Hong Kong), Deak (India), Nadia (Egypt), Greta (Great Britain), Ellen (Israel), Rashida (India), and many others who sang for me in parks, playgrounds, and sandboxes.

Contents

THE LAUGHING BABY

I. *Reasons for Rhymes*

Why Nursery Rhymes?

It is no coincidence that the word "nursery" has been used for centuries to mean both the fostering or developing of a child and the land in which young plants are reared until fit for transplantation. Like water and sun to plants, nursery rhymes and play can provide essential mental and physical nourishment for our babies until they have developed the maturity to be separated from us and enjoy playing by themselves.

Rhythmic sounds have been sung and chanted to babies all over the world for hundreds of years. Sounds, combined with physical contact, are used to lull babies to sleep, soothe them in times of stress, and delight them in active play. The sensations of movement and the

4 Reasons for Rhymes

power of music and voice all help to develop the baby's nervous system, giving a sense of harmony which the baby will associate with nursery rhymes for years to come. In addition, sensations that arise from body movement help to stimulate the part of the brain that is involved in making words. The degree of novelty which a baby is exposed to in our society makes nursery rhymes even more important in providing continuity and familiarity for the baby.

Nursery rhymes create a comfortable framework in which the baby can explore his body, sensations, and his environment without excessive stress. The amount of stimulation and vigor with which nursery rhyme games are played will vary according to a baby's age and sensitivity. Games offer the baby a wonderful sense of predictability, yet the surprise endings, bounces, or peek-a-boos thrill him because they are anticipated.

Experimental psychologists interested in analyzing the value of nursery rhymes have found that they help to develop a child intellectually. Rhyming words repeated frequently begin to take on patterns for older children. These patterns of rhymed words, or even sequences of behavior of animals in a rhyme, help the child to sort out and organize things. Just as physical sensations help the brain develop ways to handle sensory input, so do nursery rhymes help the child to learn about arranging ideas into patterns.

The playing and interaction in a nursery rhyme game gives the baby a true sense of her own ability and power to integrate the world around her. A younger baby's mere smile or laugh may encourage an adult to play a rhyming game again. As the baby grows, she can participate and feel a great sense of achievement when she is involved in movements as clapping. The baby will want more, and the baby's obvious delight will be incentive for the adult to play more.

As Dr. Seuss, America's leading expert in making children laugh, writes in one of his children's books:

If you never did,
you should.
These things are fun
and fun is good.

Once you start singing nursery rhymes and playing physical games with your children, they probably won't let you stop singing them for years. Babies and children know what's good for them.

Why Play?

A woman sits in the cool shade of a palm tree, playing with her five-month-old daughter. She sings an old Spanish nursery rhyme about making tortillas, clapping her hands as she flattens her imaginary "tortita." When she comes to the verse where she twists her hands to show how beautiful they are, the baby eagerly raises her hands and gently moves them, miming the movements of her mother. The baby has heard this tune many times; she laughs in anticipation, and her mother laughs back.

Halfway across the world, in Hong Kong, a grandmother greets her friends in the village square by the temple and takes her grandson out of her backsling where she has been carrying him. She rests his body on her lap, and the other women and men turn their attention to the baby, making him laugh as their old faces crinkle into smiles. They make a clucking sound which delights the baby, and then the grandmother bounces him gently up and down, chanting, "Ho, siu, ho siu," in a rhythmic singing voice. The baby squeals with laughter and smiles. With this little song, these grandparents never fail to make the village babies and children smile. The verse translates as "beautiful smile, beautiful smile," and the babies adore it.

My observations of playing with babies in family-oriented cultures started with the birth of my first child. Being without experienced relatives to advise me on child rearing, my only recourse was books and my Chinese neighbors in the fishing village where I lived in Hong Kong. I found little reference in child-care books about playing with babies or about smiling and laughter, except that babies like it. So I turned towards the parents and grandparents around me, and watched. From my apartment roof I observed the Chinese grandmothers taking care of the babies while the mothers washed clothes or vegetables at the village pump. The grandmothers played with the babies, talked and laughed with each other, or just sat quietly and gently bounced the babies on their laps. When I would go to the beach for a walk or run in the late afternoon, I found these same women sitting under the trees in the shade, and they expressed their approval of my breast-feeding my baby. They asked if they could take my daughter from me as if I were giving them a gift for a half hour, and the laughing and singing would start anew. Zoë, my baby, loved it. Before long, these women began to look at me as a mother and not as a foreigner. Some would ask if they could take Zoë for a walk and then play with her for a while with the other grandmothers and babies. As I watched, it was always the same. Different types of movement, different singing voices ranging from soft to raucous, and the babies smiled and laughed in response. If one of the old women grew too loud, and the baby began to fret, then the grandmother would gently bounce the baby into a peaceful state again. No bottles, no rubber pacifiers, no strollers. Just touch, movement, and voices.

The Way We Were

In traditional agricultural societies, children spent more time in physical contact with their mothers, fathers, or close kin. Children were typically carried around until age two, three, or four, and breast-fed for several years. Sleeping alone was uncommon. The extended family took the pressure off the parents to care for the child, so more time was devoted to the physical care of the baby, including play.

A look at contemporary traditional societies gives us a clearer picture of what was biologically intended for the parent-infant relationship. We have forgotten these laws of nature in our attempts to compromise with the demands of living in a technological society. Child abuse statistics glaringly question the ability of our society to cope with children. Why is the child becoming an object of hostility rather than a source of continuing delight?

By learning to play with babies, we experience the easy relationship that can come when we listen to their sensitive and varied needs. In order to do this, however, we have to free ourselves from society's expectations of how parents are supposed to act with babies. The constraints of daily time schedules, achievement goals, and the work ethic in our society do not make space for playing for pure pleasure.

In contrast to traditional societies, we are living in an artificial, media-dominated culture. It is difficult to hear our intuition when we are deafened by the noise of our technological society. Yet intuition is a powerful tool which guides parents and caretakers in caring for their young. By using our intuition, we can ensure that we will be supplying our babies' needs for successful biological development.

While playing with my two babies, I noticed subtle changes over the months. When I played regularly with them, when we laughed together, touched each other, looked in each other's eyes, I found that they became happier and "easier." This play reinforces the parent-infant bond. It is easy to respond with enjoyment to a baby who smiles and laughs with you. The negative effects of low-frequency smiling and laughter can cause tension and, when held, the baby may respond with crying and increased tension. The "ricochet" effect of baby smiling and then parent smiling and back again should not be underestimated.

Parents are vulnerable to fears about not doing "the right thing" according to experts, but this fear dissolves with concrete evidence of happy, bright babies resulting from trust in our own intuition.

We played many games together, we pat-a-caked, we rode-a-cock-horse. The clapping and bouncing or the rhythms of the nursery rhymes created a sense of comfort as we went through familiar routines.

Cultures around the world have rhymes which are sung to children while playing with them. Besides giving the child a sense of ease at hearing the same words and rhythms repeated, the sound corresponds with the movements and makes the playing more fun. It also helps the baby later to vocalize and understand words, and, rather than actually teaching language in formal manner, nursery rhymes assist language acquisition in a natural way.

Play for Health

Why do babies need certain types of play for healthy development? There is a growing body of evidence which indicates that holding and carrying the infant turn out to be two of the most important factors responsible for the infant's normal mental and social development. According to Dr. A. Jean Ayres, "without a great deal of full body play, the child does not get the kind of sensory input that is necessary to develop the brain as a whole. In addition, he will not have the experiences of mastery necessary for normal personality development."

Play offers us a chance to be with our babies in a delightful way, while providing them with the stimulation they require. Very specific neurological development occurs when an infant is stimulated through movement. Scientists of various disciplines have been attracted to testing the limits of animals and humans by exposing them to unnatural environments and observing the effects. While the human being can adapt and survive in appalling conditions, the human's well-being seems to be based upon certain requirements. If, as an infant, these requirements in the form of biological needs are not met, the development of the child will be less than perfect. The needs for stimulation, corresponding to the infant's inner drive for certain types of body movement, ensure the development of a child more at peace with herself and the environment around her.

Every traditional culture in the world instinctively understands the necessity of movement and play with infants, as do many higher species of the animal kingdom. Living according to the laws of biology and nature does not mean that we have to live in nature. A deeper understanding of infant development necessitates giving a greater emphasis to play than our society now does.

Unlike babies in more traditional societies, our babies spend a great deal of their time left on their own. The antisocial restrictions in our adult-oriented culture mean that we are spending not only less time touching our babies but less time even being with our children. Mothers and fathers are generally not allowed to bring young children to work; day care at the workplace is very unusual. Breast-feeding mothers are either discouraged or actively forbidden to bring nursing infants to their place of employment. The use of playpens, cribs, car seats, baby bouncers and mechanical swings all help the parent considerably when there is other work to be done; but these devices are also wedges which further separate our babies from us.

Except at parks or organized meetings with other parents, we do not learn from observation of other parents' interaction with their infants, and for new parents to learn what is natural can be a very difficult task indeed. As parents or caretakers we read books on child care, and most of the time laughter and play is given little if any importance. It is assumed that the reader will simply know about things like that.

This book has been written with the hope that by playing with our babies in ways which bring out their laughter and joy from being in tune with their biological needs, we will learn to listen carefully, not only to our babies but to ourselves.

Who Took the Nature Out of Children?

Physicians have said that young parents have lost the skill to raise children. We notice many children who are devoting themselves to autistic games—assembly of plastic toys, game machines or personal computers. As a result, many are suffering from psychosomatic disorders.

Children have lost their intrinsic nature, fellowship and adventure in exchange for affluence. They can no longer have actual experience in many cases and must be satisfied with pseudo-experience of indirect experience. This may be a terrible thing. Many people who are now of middle age or older were brought up in the midst of nature. With the rapid proliferation of urbanization, we, the grown-ups have failed to include nature in the urban society. The children may be regarded as victims of our prosperity (*Mainichi Daily News*, Tokyo; quoted in the *San Jose Mercury News*, June 1984).

Play brings us back to nature, even if the playing occurs within the confines of a city apartment. It is a universal characteristic, found in all cultures and animals of higher species, and it is one way to grow closer to the nature of our children. Think about the lives of many children today, and how their daily activities are organized around parents' working lives. Day care is the norm for the majority of children, and television is watched an average of 27 hours per week by the two-to-five age group. Learning from real life is easily replaced by television and video games, with the result that children are spending less time than ever in the natural, physical world. Discontented children are rarely comfortable with the tangible world around them and feel uneasy when interacting with their environment.

A child's inner peace, security, and happiness rest upon her moving at her own pace, both physically and mentally. There is a natural order to child development. This order unfolds, as nature intended, to allow the child to receive stimulation and challenges when she is ready, and to seek them out when she is comfortable with the world she has already interacted with. Like the concentric rings which surround a pebble dropped into a pond, the child's world expands slowly, and her ability to increase her world depends upon the security and mastery she already feels with her current limited world.

If we slip into the flow of an infant's development and perceive and meet his needs, the reward will inevitably be one of harmony. Experiments, both clinical and personal, demonstrate that responding quickly to a baby's needs will produce a baby who cries less frequently in the second half of his first year. A baby uses signals and cries to express his needs. If these are ignored in an effort to "save time" or "get things done," what is a minor nuisance now will probably grow to take more time and energy when the baby is older. The more physical contact a baby receives early in life, the more independent he will be later.

When a pattern different from the one nature has already programmed for children is imposed on a child, it will be found that nature cannot be fooled. We could find aberrations which will reveal themselves in our children at some later stage, either as physical or psychological disorders. There could be a loss of the contentment and at-one-with-the-world feeling that goes along with the child who has been allowed to unfold at his own pace. Learning problems at school, hyperactivity, over-aggressiveness, or a lack of physical coordination are some of the ways that children deal with an inability to integrate what they see, hear, feel, smell and taste.

Playing with movement can help the baby to learn about himself and the world around him and feel the pleasure which comes from being able to organize the sensations he is receiving. There is a direct link between the physical stimulation an infant needs and the growth of neural pathways—those links in the brain which allow it to smoothly organize information and use it. Or, as Dr. Ayres observes,

> Sensations are "food" or nourishment for the nervous system. Every muscle, joint, vital organ, bit of skin, and sense organ in the head sends sensory inputs to the brain. Every sensation is a form of information. The nervous system uses this information to produce responses that adapt the body and mind to that information. Without a good supply of many kinds of sensations, the nervous system cannot develop adequately. The brain needs a continuous variety of sensory nourishment to develop and then to function (p. 33).

•CHAPTER 2•

Sensory Integration Through Playing

The most important stimulation is touch. Among animals, lack of touching can be life-threatening.

—M. Samuels & N. Samuels

I nfants require sensory stimulation of varying levels during different stages of growth. Touch is one type of stimulation which, to a newborn infant, initiates most innate reflexes. Touch a baby's cheek, and she will turn her mouth toward that direction in search of a nipple. Reflexes are based upon touch which not only develops emotional security but actually develops the brain and the nervous system. Touching also influences the immunological system, neurological development, weight gain and mental functioning in babies. Visual and auditory stimulation are not enough. Beyond mobiles hanging over cribs and music boxes, we need to teach our infants through their entire sensory systems.

Is it possible that we are out of touch with touching? Sensory integration specialist Laura Sobel, in Santa Barbara, California, has taught over one thousand parents the basics about touching their infants, and the demand for her classes is great. Clearly, parents are finding a need to learn the fundamental requirements for healthy, happy babies. Sobel explains to parents,

> We need to give infants touch in the skin sense as well as in the deeper sense of massage, creating impulses in muscles and joints which send messages into the brain. Movement through space is another system which needs stimulation, such as carrying or swinging in the air, or being rocked.

Sensory integration (or sensory-motor integration) refers to the organization for use of all types of sensory input that goes into the brain. There are nerve cells near the surface of the skin that perceive sensations of touch, pain and temperature. Another sense detects the pull of gravity and the movement of the body in relation to earth. Other nerve cells are around joints, in muscles, in the palms of hands and the soles of the feet.

The nervous system is the interconnected network of nerve cells that is distributed throughout the body. The brain is made up of nerve cells, as is the spinal cord. This is the central nervous system. The nerve cells outside this system are spread throughout the skin, muscles, joints, internal organs and sense organs of the head.

Vision, hearing, taste, smell and touch are the traditional senses, but sensory integration therapy focuses on the importance of full body movements that provide tactile stimulation (skin), vestibular stimulation (gravity and equilibrium), and proprioceptive stimulation (joints and muscles).

The brain receives sensory input from the nerve cells and organizes and interprets this information. It then sends signals for the body to move in response. This is followed by sensory feedback. An example of sensory integration can be illustrated with a child and a bowl of apples. The child sees the apples (visual sensory input, which is quickly integrated with information from associated areas of the brain which tell the child from past experiences what he is seeing); he reaches for an apple and grasps it (motor response); and bites into it (sensory feedback of touching the apple, feeling the weight of it and tasting it).

The great majority of all learning in the first few years of life involves sensory input and movements within the child's body. According to Sobel,

> The way very young children learn is different from the way adults learn. We learn through our eyes and ears. Infants learn through their bodies about their environment. The stimulation they experience with their bodies teaches their brains what it is.

Ayres, an occupational therapist (whose clinical research has led to the present understanding of sensory integration), explains further that sensory integration

> begins in the womb as the fetal brain senses the movements of the mother's body. An enormous amount of sensory integration must occur and develop to produce crawling and standing up, and this happens in the first year of life. Childhood play leads to a lot of sensory integration as the child organizes the sensations of his body and gravity along with sight and sound.

A baby develops sensory integration by interacting with his environment and responding to it. When a baby has mastered one response to a sensory experience, such as reaching for something he sees, he will move on to more complex responses, such as crawling toward a toy that is out of reach.

Within every child there is a great inner drive to develop sensory integration. Nature directs from within such skills as holding the head erect, sitting, creeping, standing and, finally walking. This has been described by Joseph Pearce as a blueprint which unfolds period by period, and this period of "intent" seeks out the "content" for that period. This occurs at a genetically timed pace, and each new stage will unfold at the time appropriate to the child. After millions of years of refinement, nature does not program for failure.

The human being is designed to enjoy those things that promote development of the brain. We naturally seek sensations that help to organize our brains. Children love to be picked up, rocked, hugged; they play, jump, stretch themselves with challenges at the playground and dare the waves to get them wet on the beach. They are spurred to move because the sensations of movement nourish their brains.

The child searches his environment for opportunities to develop. In the sequence of development, the child needs to develop building blocks that become the basis for more complex and mature growth. Sensations of gentle movement help to organize the brain, and rocking a young infant has immediate calming effects. When my four-year-old is upset by a bad dream, or is tired or overstimulated, a few minutes of rocking seem to give her peace.

And Fun Is Good

Have you ever noticed how much young children love to roughhouse with parents or play piggy-back, and how when you stop they beg for more? This type of play provides sensory input from the body and from gravity receptors in our inner ears. Sensations that make a child happy tend to be integrating.

" 'Fun' is the child's word for sensory integration," according to neurologist Jean Ayres. It gives a great deal of satisfaction to organize sensations and even more satisfaction to respond to those sensations with adaptive responses that are more complex than before.

Nature has intended that playing with our babies and children can create more integrated children who are better able to handle stress and change, and contributes to the early development of a stronger bond between parents and children. Surely, everyone plays with his or her offspring, but in varying ways. Some are more imaginative and have a greater variety of games, and others prefer a less stimulating, no-touch type of playing.

Babies love movement. After all, they were moving continuously during their time in the mother's womb. The sudden stillness of a crib and no physical contact must be a frightening experience for an infant.

It is an unnatural achievement for the human baby to spend his life in a crib. He is in no way adjusted to the crib; rather, his wish to be carried around becomes clearly evident again and again. Calming by rocking or pacifiers is reminiscent of the time when mother and child were physically more closely associated (Albrecht Peiper, 1963).

In all primate species other than humans, infants are in almost continuous contact with their mothers during the early months of life. The species that have the most complex skills need play the most, while species with less complex skills usually mature rapidly, and need less time with the mother. In most animal species the main function of play is probably to develop strengths and skills in the young in preparation for life-and-death sit-uations in adult life. We can speculate that it was probably the same for humans at one time, but is no longer vital for our survival. Our brains and nervous systems still depend, however, on certain types of stimulation which occur naturally in play. Through play the child obtains the sensory input from her body and from gravity that is essential for both motor and emotional development. Children need a lot of play when they are young.

In traditional cultures mothers carry their babies around on their backs, and often babies spend most of their first few years seeing the world from their mother's, aunt's, or grandmother's back. While this is possible in our society when the baby is small, it becomes increasingly difficult to continue to carry our infants or be near them as they grow older, especially for working parents who must be away from the home. Movement through playing is some compensation for the decreased amount of time that our babies are held.

Since babies love play of a certain type and express their enjoyment through smiles and laughter, the types of play and games which most please them can offer us a clue to what they need. Nature has cleverly wired us in such a manner. Babies seem to enjoy thrills and surprises in their games. When they are ready for greater stimulation, they will show signs of boredom with the gentle movement and will eagerly delight in slightly more vigorous movement which will stretch them in the way that they require. The baby sets the pace, however, and it is important that we show great awareness for personal preferences in play. The laughter and smiles are the critical factors in this observation. When babies smile and laugh they become livelier, more animated and more lovable. Parents are more likely to interact with them because there is more feedback and fun in the relationship.

In such interaction you will help your baby respond to you and the world around her. There is a dance of interaction when that which the parent does influences the baby, and vice versa. Smiling and laughter keep this interaction strong.

As the baby grows older, she needs increasingly vigorous stimulation. The stimulation that a baby gets when a parent is trying to get her to laugh is usually quite vigorous—more vigorous than the stimulation she normally gets. The games in this book emphasize active, physical games in association with the nursery rhymes. Lifting in the air, bouncing on the knee, hand clapping and surprise endings are all ways to give your baby stimulation as well as immense pleasure. And who can resist wanting to hold a happy baby?

How to Play

After years of observation of infants at play in a pre-technological, preagricultural society in South America, Jean Liedloff said, "The infant's business in arms is to have experiences which will ready him for further development toward self-reliance" (1977, p. 161). Young children will often actively seek out the thrills of slightly fearful situations, such as swinging on swings, wading in the surf, and jumping from high places. Have you ever heard the squeals of delight and fear when a small child runs from a wave on the beach and immediately goes back to wait for the next one? As Liedloff noticed, "the secret of the attraction is in the safety zone."

The exploration and excitement of a possibly fearful, unknown situation, while still pleasurably in safety, allows for the stimulation which babies seek as the normal unfolding of their physical development occurs. It is the wonderful laughter and integrating rewards of playing with babies which indicate that play is one of nature's keys to healthy human development.

Since laughter is your baby's way of telling you what he enjoys, pay close attention to which games succeed in making your baby laugh and to what degree they succeed. This laughter is the final judge of what is or is not a good game, rather than any particular theories about play which you may have. Many parents know this instinctively and don't have to read about it in a book, but others may become overly intellectual about playing with their babies and may need to be reminded of the simplicity of playing.

As long as your baby is giggling and laughing, don't be afraid to bounce, lift and swing him. The danger comes when we, as parents, enjoy ourselves so much in these games that we stop watching for alarm signals.

When the baby looks nervous, frets, or doesn't laugh, some parents become annoyed that their child is not appreciating their efforts. This is when overstimulation can occur, and a game can quickly accelerate into a frightening experience for the infant.

If any of these danger signals appear, then change pace, and comfort the baby by a gentle rhythmic rocking, or just hugging. With practice you will learn his limits and be able to foresee impending tears caused by overstimulation. Moderation in infant play is wonderful, but an excess will only tire her, and she will at some point proclaim "Enough!"

The Child's Rhythm

Listening to advice or books on baby care should take a back seat while you quietly observe your baby and let her tell you when she is ready for stimulation and laughing, and when she just wants peace to be by herself. Trusting in a baby's innate sense of development will let you respond with certain types of play, and careful attention to her laughter and subtle (or not so subtle) early distress signals will let you know how you are doing. Nature is extremely trustworthy while the fetus is developing for nine months, and just because the baby is now outside doesn't mean that she suddenly has become cut off from her inner drives.

The biological plan of nature allows the baby to develop at his own pace, and distress or crying while at play usually occurs when this pace has not been honored. When he has had enough stimulation and needs to shut off for a while, he will certainly let you know, if you are observant.

I remember the first few lessons I had with my daughter Zoë in her early months, and what she taught me has never been forgotten. We would take her to certain types of parties, with a handful of people, quiet music, and a fairly peaceful atmosphere. She would blissfully fall asleep after watching for a while, and people would make comments about how lucky we were to have such a "good" baby. (To many nonparents, a good baby is a very quiet baby.) Thinking that she was a sociable child, we brought her to other social gatherings, one of which turned out to be wilder, louder, and more crowded. She wasn't smiling, but since she didn't look unhappy, we stayed. By the time we took her home, she let us know we had overextended our stay. A howling rose from within her and lasted for more than an hour—most unusual behavior for her. It was a shattering noise to us; she had been overstimulated, and we didn't heed her signals.

It took a few repetitions of this for us to realize what her limits were. We respect her innate response to stimulation even now that she is four-and-a-half, and the result is a composed, happy child. When circumstances have prevented us from respecting her needs, she has whined, complained, and become irritable, behaviors which many people curiously think is normal.

Babies' interest and tolerance for playing change all the time, depending upon their mood, stage of development, and even on physical aspects such as teething or the weather. Just as in food taste, what may be wonderful this week may be boring the next, and the baby will certainly let you know.

I gave Maya, my two-year-old daughter, frequent massages as a baby. She went through a long period, however, when she refused any massage at all; her joy in being able to move meant that she wouldn't sit still. Nursery rhymes and games then became very important to keep our interaction strong, because we no longer had the eye contact and focus that came from massaging her. Now that she is nearly three she enjoys massages again, but only at certain times. Big bounces and high lifts are her preference now, the sillier the better.

The birth itself will also affect the type of stimulation a baby likes. A premature birth or a long, difficult labor with medical intervention may increase the baby's sensitivity to touch. Touching is what every baby requires to develop the nervous system, but gentleness and low-level stimulation may be required for the first few months. If there is a part of your baby's body where he obviously does not like to be touched, don't force it. Keep trying gently over the weeks, so he eventually associates touch with pleasure. Sometimes just laying your hand on that part while he is sleeping can help overcome this.

As children grow older, they increase the degree of stimulation and risk that they can endure very gradually and prudently. A good example of this can be seen in young children wading in the surf. Early on, babies hesitantly get their toes wet while holding an adult's hand. Older children will often wade up to their ankles, observe the wave patterns, and go screaming and laughing back to safety when the waves come crashing in. Most of the danger is under control, but they go back for more. They laugh and scream when they get such a thrill but rarely go beyond the depth of their knees. They naturally seek an element of risk within a controlled environment.

Games with babies can teach us a great deal about ourselves, and much of our own ego is expressed when playing with them. We might be surprised if we could see ourselves objectively. Some parents get too involved in the games, so much so that they get annoyed and even hurt when the baby has had enough and starts crying. The parent didn't pick up any of the early warning signals and then may say something like, "Well, if you're only going to cry when I play with you, I won't bother." This is not unusual and has more to do with our own attitude and less to do with the baby's own natural pace—which will lead to harmony when sensitively observed.

Playful Tips

A few points to remember when playing with your baby:

1. Vary the play for interest. Change the tempo of a particular nursery rhyme and keep the suspense longer before the bump, tickle or lift. Babies love surprises, so be inventive!

2. Vary the baby's physical stimulation. The more variety in play, the more it contributes to development. When the brain reacts to movement, it eventually pays less attention if it is feeling the same movement over and over again. If we want to encourage brain development, advises Laura Sobel, change the sensations—not just in play, but in how we carry babies, how we feed them, the materials we give them to play with. Get the baby to know where she is in space with rhymes and games for up, down, left, right and upside-down. Play around with gravity.

3. Let siblings play with the baby, and learn from them. Initially a sister may play with the baby in a way which is rougher than you might want, however. It may be appropriate to suggest something like, "Look into the baby's eyes when you play." This rapport usually focuses the sibling to the baby rather than playing for the parent's attention. Eye contact is just as important for adults when playing with children.

4. Because many of us, as new parents, are not used to playing such games and making funny noises, try to let go of your inhibitions while playing. The baby usually adores the silly, fun-loving side of parents, and the more

you sing and play, the easier it is for the playfulness in you to blossom.

5. Use different inflections when saying nursery rhymes, especially using animal sounds or different tones. As the baby grows older, these sounds will fascinate her, and eventually she will learn to articulate and make sounds to imitate you. Please don't "explain" to your baby why you are playing. Abstract thinking and reasoning come *after* a child has a concrete knowledge of her body, many years later.

6. Don't be too gentle with your baby. A lesson learned from my four-year-old is that jumping on the bed, making the baby bounce into the air a few inches, gets the baby to laugh real belly laughs. The baby's joy, which comes from experiencing stronger gravity and movement sensations, and integrating them is your reward. Experiment, and then observe her closely. She will probably want more than you had expected.

7. Always encourage the baby's initiatives. One way to do this is by making an exaggerated reaction to the baby miming you, or perhaps clapping or touching your own nose during a feature rhyme. The baby will love your reaction and will do it again if you make your responses big and funny. It gives a great sense of power to a baby to be able to interact in such a way.

8. The older a baby gets, the more stimulation the baby will want and need. You can lift higher, tickle harder, surprise more, and the baby will be happier. The baby innately seeks challenges to stretch her physical and mental capacities.

9. Don't overdo it. Knowing when to stop is perhaps the most difficult aspect of playing. Too much intense play is disturbing and disorienting, and the baby may cry. Or, if she has had too much, she will either begin to fret slightly, or just stop smiling.

10. Enjoy yourself. The baby will know if you are having fun, or only playing from a sense of duty.

·CHAPTER 3·

Food for Thought

While movement and play will nourish your baby and help him develop beautifully and happily, the source of energy which gives him the ability to kick his legs with delight must also be attended to. No matter how much love and care you might give a plant, it will not be sturdy unless it is nourished with good soil, water, and sunlight. Our daily bread—our food—is a vital link in the chain of development of our young which cannot be overlooked. Taking responsibility for our baby's health and well-being embraces all forms of sustenance, internal as well as external.

Diet and Play

The food we eat, like the way we play, allows us to be more in touch with our biological requirements. In a sense we are a new breed living in a technological age and have veered away from many of the practices to which our bodies are most adapted. The air we breathe, the water we drink, the amount of chemicals in our environment, the type of exercise we get, and of course the food we eat are all very different from those our ancestors used. Our national diet is causing significant health problems in the United States today, and people find it difficult to follow their natural instincts with food. Intuition is strongest when our bodies are healthy, and a wholesome diet will help us to create a more balanced way of living.

For centuries mankind has owed its existence largely to the family of cereal grains. Rice, wheat, millet, oats, rye, maize, and buckwheat still form the basis of most of the world population's diet. However, since World War II, the use of grains in the Western world—and their quality—has diminished due to the reliance on chemicals in food processing. Grains are now largely refined, adding to our expense and robbing the grains of most of their nutritional value. The 1977 report on "Dietary Goals for the United States," issued by the United States Senate Select Committee on Nutrition and Human Needs, suggests that for optimum health Americans should consume more fresh vegetables, whole grains, fish, and fruits, and decrease their intake of sugar, processed foods, and saturated fats as in meat and dairy products.

Eating a wide range of foods, preferably grown locally and seasonally, can offer a well-balanced diet which can strengthen our bodies and bring us closer to the rhythms of nature. If we don't have the time to eat and cook well, then we probably won't have time to play well.

Traditional Foods

Imagine a time when there were no doctors in your area, no pediatricians, no milk formula on the supermarket shelves, no pharmaceutical companies, no aspirin. The nearest health practitioner (nurse, witch doctor, shaman, or herbalist) might have been a few days' ride away. Your support when your child was not well came from your parents, grandparents, neighbors, and the vast storehouse of information which is carefully filed in the library of tradition. Beliefs handed down after centuries of observation and experimentation were needed for survival. There was no one you could hand over your sick child to and say, "Make her better." Tradition permeated life and gave parents the strength to take care of their offspring, farmers the knowledge to grow their crops, weavers the skills to fashion garments, and poets the inspiration to write.

Every culture in the world has traditions concerning the dietary practices of its people. This wisdom is founded on an understanding of the environment in which people lived, and helps the people live in as healthy a manner as possible. It is impossible to divorce the happiness of your baby from the food that you eat, whether it is directly ingested by the fetus, or through your breast milk, or the formula which you feed her.

When I was living in Shek O, a fishing village in Hong Kong, a friend from the village, Kam Lin, or Golden Lotus, began to offer me advice and admonitions as to what I should be eating or avoiding during the months I nursed my first daughter. She would say "too *leung*" to me every time I drank iced tea, or would shake her head, furrow her brow, and start clucking when she saw me eating tofu (bean curd) daily. "*Leung*" is Cantonese for cool, but I also heard her say "*tai yit*" when she saw me eating too much deep-fried food, which, according to Chinese food understanding, is "heating" food, creating too much stimulation in the body. I began to explore these concepts, as I had a great deal of respect for her; her children were exceedingly healthy, as she was, and as were her brothers and sisters, her mother and great-grandmother.

Diet was considered to be of crucial importance to the health of a nursing baby, and I wanted more detail about Chinese concepts of food. With Kam Lin as the go-between, I began to interview the grandmothers and great-grandmothers in the village about their dietary practices while nursing, as I knew that they might be the librarians of tradition on this subject. Anyone younger, in general, preferred to "go modern," and had forgotten many of the old ways. It appeared as no coincidence to me that there was a much higher occurrence of weaker children among those women, and more colds, diarrhea, stomach troubles, and less resistance in general. This was later confirmed by the older women.

Kam Lin, along with the older generation of women, applauded my breast-feeding, while the younger women told me that they preferred the bottle for its convenience. I realized that the wisdom of the two older generations in the village—the women who had lived in what is now The People's Republic of China and raised large and healthy children—was not being heeded. As I learned more, I began cautiously asking for advice and then asking questions outright about the breast-feeding tradition. Soon I was invited into homes; the older women were more than eager to tell me about their experiences. In an uninhibited fashion, these crinkly-eyed and laughing women would grab their breasts and reenact their youth as they were relating their stories.

One great-grandmother of eighty years, a sunworn woman who has been living in Hong Kong for thirty years, related the following:

"I had nine children, but we were very poor. I breast-fed my children for four years each, although some of the women in the village breast-fed their children until they were eight years old. We did not have enough food. As for problems with our milk, we had no choice but to breast-feed, so were very, very careful to make good milk. We had nothing else."

Kao-Mui, a broad-smiling, gold-toothed woman, was in her sixties when she left the mainland for Hong Kong. Her babies were nursed for several years each, and she was convinced that their strength came from the food she ate and the food she gave them in childhood.

A seventy-five-year-old from another part of the mainland had raised her children on breast milk for four years each. "We were very poor and did not have enough food to give to the children. I ate fish, brown rice, vegetables and pickles, and soy bean products. If someone got sick, there were no doctors and no other medicine. We would to up to the hills and collect herbs. We ate no fat during nursing, and seldom ate fruit. If the baby became sick or upset when the mother ate a particular food, she would never eat that again, especially if it caused stomach troubles."

The consistent theme heard from the women I interviewed, even though they were from widely dispersed parts of China, was the importance of being cautious with food. Chinese traditional food theory defines food as the best medicine, and it was accepted that the food eaten by the mother had a direct relationship to the health of the breast-fed baby.

Seasonal foods were stressed. The older women observed that foods eaten out of season by the younger generations in Hong Kong seemed to cause the body to become unbalanced, inviting disorders of various kinds. Seasonal foods sustain the body at particular times. It was felt that eating imported foods out of season was not appropriate for either nursing mothers or, less critically, for growing children.

The point that was driven home to me was that a respect for food and for its power to provide strength and health is taking a back seat to the current attitude, which is based primarily on taste. It is only in the last few decades that industrial countries have begun to wonder about the connection between cancer, heart disease, hypertension, and diet.

What can we learn from these traditions, and the ones which we have inherited? Look into the food traditions of your ancestors, whether they be Latin, Asian, European, Middle Eastern, or Native American, and you will find that food is linked to health and behavior.

I started investigating traditional food concepts when I was living in Central America, and began to discover an older generation, not brought up on french fries and hamburgers, who still have this information intact. I again found theories of heating and cooling foods, classifications of food which are thought to develop strong children, and of foods that weaken. Goals of harmony and balance are universal, and it was felt that "modern," that is, processed foods, did not fulfill basic requirements for good health.

We can accept that nature's laws for the development of children will lead us to have happy, harmonious children, but many people find the link between food and behavior difficult to grasp. In the last decade, as we move into an era where fast foods, high fat, and high sugar are more commonplace for our children than a bowl of simple oatmeal, these natural laws are being ignored, and parents spend money on psychologists and learning specialists before they look to the candy wrappers lying on the bedroom floor.

It is known that drugs and alcohol can cause emotional and behavioral disorders, but sugar, white flour products, and chemical additives have proven to be just as powerful in their effects on the behavior of our children. Anger, tantrums, whining, and crying are not the signs of a healthy, emotionally balanced child. If we begin to examine closely the effects of these foods on children, we will begin to discover some interesting facts about blood sugar levels and behavior.

In *Food, Teens and Behavior*, Barbara Reed found that in her career as a probation officer, the majority of people who were getting into trouble showed signs of hypoglycemia, or other blood sugar disorders. She began testing her ideas of nutrition on the teenagers who found themselves in court, and was surprised, as were the judges, at her enormous success. She encouraged the young people on probation to eat a diet emphasizing fresh fruits and vegetables, whole grains, lean meats, and fish, with a total ban on sugar, white flour products, and chemicals. A remarkably high number of her subjects managed to stay out of the courts and lead productive lives. Reed summarized her philosophy:

My message everywhere has remained the same: a simple diet of whole foods, eaten as fresh, unprocessed and pure as possible, is absolutely necessary in order to give the brain and the rest of the central nervous system what it needs to function properly. On the other hand, ignoring the nutrition of the body is the most dangerous mistake one can make. A malnourished central nervous system will inevitably lead to serious physical and behavioral problems, problems which no amount of medication or psychiatry can touch (1983:38).

Reed goes on to advise:

It is especially the parents of young people who ought to be concerned with this. Almost every parent wants a better world for his or her children than the one we find ourselves in today. The rise of crime and violence, the abuse of women, children and the elderly, make us all wonder if there will be a world for the young generation to inherit. What is important for parents to know is that by doing something very basic and simple—by making sure that your kids are well-nourished—you can make progress toward solving the problems of criminality, delinquency, violence and mental illness, and even help reduce the tremendous toll that crime and rehabilitation of convicts takes on the resources of society (40).

Reed illustrates a powerful argument for such a diet in her explanation of the biochemistry of crime, relating the role of improper diet in the malfunction of the brain. The brain is the most important organ in the body but the most vulnerable as well. It can store no energy, it survives only a few minutes without oxygen or glucose, and it decays very rapidly under adverse conditions. When something is wrong with the body, the brain suffers first. It is directly affected by diet because of its vulnerability to its molecular environment. Behavior—the visible consequence of brain function—is, therefore, strongly influenced by diet.

According to Reed, many Americans have blood sugar levels which are too low to meet the brain's needs. This phenomenon is widespread because of the radical change in the diet of Western societies, a change which has taken place within the last eight decades of human history and is based on the extreme increase in sugar consumption.

As the blood sugar level drops, the cerebrum—the area of the brain responsible for thought, learning, and moral and social behavior—starts to shut down, and the brain diverts its dwindling energy resources to the brain stem, which controls the more primitive responses, the drives for food and sex, aggressive and defensive instincts, and basic bodily functions.

Once I began to draw the connection between food and behavior, in combination with the external factors involved, I became sensitive to my children and the effects that food had on them. I can see clearly that an even, long-burning supply of whole grain carbohydrates gives my children (and myself) a peaceful, smooth energy for daily activities. When this is disturbed by an excessive amount of sugar in a special treat, or misuse of sweeteners (even honey, which is 99 percent sucrose), I can see weepy, irritable children soon after. Other aspects of their food, such as too much salt, or too little salt, also have a visible effect. This is different for every individual, and it must be stressed that no one diet is good for everyone.

The key to our daily food is balance and sensitivity. Just as a baby requires specific stimulation for healthy development and happiness, so does she require nutritional balance. We have in our power the capability of offering the best strengthening foods to our babies and children. When we play with children we are aware of nature's plans for them. When we feed our children, we should have the same awareness.

II. *Rhymes for Verse and Play*

•CHAPTER 4•

Rocking Songs

L ullabies, used for thousands of years, have passed the test of time. Just as the rocking motion tends to be soothing, so the slow, gentle, rhythmic sounds of a lullaby bring peace to a baby. In addition to calming a baby, carrying and rocking provide sensations that are essential building blocks for later sensations and future body movements. The word *lullaby* derives from the Middle English *lully*, or *lulla*, meaning a repetition of "lu lu" or similar sounds to sing a child to sleep. Going back even further, the word in Latin is *lallare*, "to sing to sleep."

A Stanford University study suggests that premature babies who are rocked mechanically showed fewer signs of irritability, were alert more often, and had fewer occasions of interrupted breathing during sleep than similar babies who stayed in an ordinary incubator. Other studies of laboratory animals suggest to scientists that lack of such movement after birth can impair the early development of the brain.

Rocking songs can be powerful projections of a world that we wish to bring to our children. The words and melodies wriggle through our rational armor and can make us stop for a moment and fully embrace and enjoy being with our babies. The songs carry with them tenderness and love, using images of moons, nests, and other comforting aspects of nature.

At night I watch the tensions of the day dissolve within minutes of a rocking song. I know that Zoë, my eldest, has had a particularly hectic day when she asks for a bedtime song instead of a story. The magic of one of her favorites, "Hush 'n Bye," soon carries her off to sleep. I find that singing songs that have been sung by countless women before me offers a sense of continuity and comfort to both of us.

SWEET WATER ROLLING (South Carolina)

Sweet water rolling,
Sweet water roll,
Rolling from the fountain,
Sweet water roll.

UNE POULE BLANCHE (French lullaby)

Une poule blanche	A white hen
Qui est dans le grange	Sitting in the barn
A poudu son petit coco	Laid her little egg
Pour bebe qui fait dodo	For baby who is sleeping
Dodo, dodelinetto,	Dodo, dodelinetto,
Dodo, dodelino.	Dodo, dodelino.

HOPI LULLABY (Hopi Indians)

Puva . . . puva . . . puva,
In the trail the beetles
On each other's backs are sleeping,
So on mine, my baby, thou.
Puva . . . puva . . . puva.

PIMA WIND SONG (Pima Indians)

Far on the desert ridges
Stands the cactus;
Lo, the blossoms swaying
To and fro, the blossoms swaying, swaying.

THE BALLAD OF DOWNAL BAUN
(Domhnal Ban, Irish)

The moon-cradle's rocking and rocking,
Where a cloud and a cloud goes by:
Silently rocking and rocking,
The moon-cradle out in the sky.

HATI JHULARE (Indian lullaby)

Hati jhulare,
Ba, pani khai phulare

Hati Jhulu thae,
Lasara pasara, kia kanda khai baku
Kahnai jhulai,
Jashoda kolare, khira kale khai baku.

Little elephant swaying,
Growing up breathing pure air
    and eating fresh branches,
Little elephant,
Swaying this way and that way,
    to eat the heart of the kia plant.

Little Kahnai sways as well,
Nestled in Jashoda's lap, to sip a little milk.

◆◆◆

This is a very old lullaby comparing Kahnai (Krishna)
to a little elephant who sways gently in the water. In
Hindu scripture, Jashoda is Kahnai's mother.

SAMOAN ROCK-A-BYE

Moe moe pepe	Rock-a-bye baby
Tumutumu o laua	On the tree tops,
A agi le matagi	When the wind blows,
E lue atu ma toe sau	The cradle will rock
A gau le lala	When the bough breaks
Pauu ai le moega	The cradle will fall
Malie oe pepe	And down will come baby
Lau faalue.	Cradle and all.

ROCK-A-BYE BABY,
THY CRADLE IS GREEN (English)

Rock-a-bye baby, thy cradle is green
Father's a nobleman, mother's a queen;
And Betty's a lady and wears a gold ring,
And Johnnie's a drummer and drums for the king.

THE SLEEPY SONG

As soon as the fire burns red and low,
And the house upstairs is still,
She sings me a queer little sleepy song,
Of sheep that go over the hill.

As one slips over and one comes next,
And one runs after behind,
The gray one's nose at the white one's tail,
The top of the hill they find.

The good little sheep run quick and soft,
Their colors are gray and white:
They follow their leader nose to tail,
For they must be home by night.

HUSH 'n BYE (South Carolina)

Hush 'n bye, don't you cry,
Oh you pretty little baby,
When you wake you'll have sweet cake,
And all the pretty little ponies,
A brown and a gray, and a black and a bay,
And all the pretty little ponies.

◆◆◆

As with all folk songs, there are many tunes for the same
song. This is an early version from South Carolina.

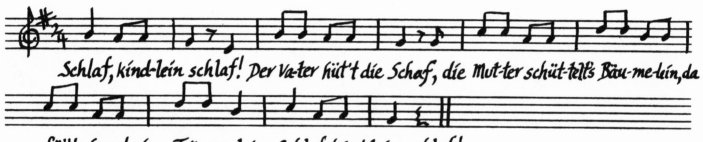

Schlaf, kind-lein schlaf! Der Va-ter hüt't die Schaf, die Mut-ter schüt-telt's Bäu-me-lein, da

fällt her-ab ein Träu-me-lein Schlaf, kind-lein, schlaf!

SCHLAF, KINDLEIN, SCHLAF

(German lullaby)

Schlaf, Kindlein, Schlaf
Dein Vater hüt't die Schaf,
Die Mutter schüttelt Bäumelein,
da fällt herab ein Träumelein.
Schlaf, Kindlein, schlaf.

Sleep, baby, sleep,
Your father takes care of the sheep,
Your mother is shaking a little tree,
A small dream falls out of it.
Sleep, little child, sleep.

SWEET AND LOW

Sweet and low, sweet and low,
  Wind of the western sea,
Low, low, breathe and blow,
  Wind of the western sea!
Over the rolling waters go,
Come from the dying moon, and blow,
  Blow him again to me;
While my little one, while my pretty one, sleeps.

Sleep and rest, sleep and rest,
  Father will come to thee soon;
Rest, rest, on mother's breast,
  Father will come to thee soon;
Father will come to his babe in the nest,
Silver sails all out of the west
  Under the silver moon;
Sleep my little one, sleep my pretty one, sleep.

—Alfred Tennyson

BAIU-BAIUSHKI-BAIU (Russian)

Baiu-baiuskhi-baiu
Kolotushek nadaiu.
Kolotushek dvadtsat' piat'
Ty pokrepche budesh spat'.

Baiu-baiuskhi-baiu
I shall pat you
Twenty-five pats lightly
So you'll sleep more
tightly.

◆◆◆

Rock the baby, patting gently on the bottom.

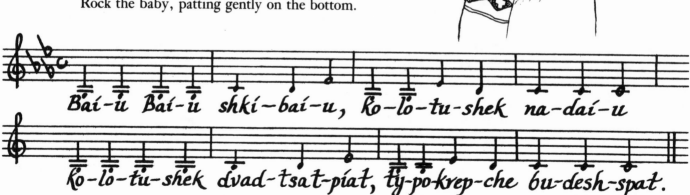

KHOD EL BEZ (Egyptian lullaby)

Khod el bez wah eskott
Khod el bez wah nam.

Take my breast and be quiet
Take my breast and sleep.

LIULI, LIULI, LIULI (Russian)

Liuli, liuli, liuli,	Liuli, liuli, liuli,
Prileteli guli,	In the pigeons flew
Seli guli na krovat',	They sat on the bed,
Stali guli vorkovat',	And they began to coo,
Tikho detku usypliat':	Quietly putting the child
	to sleep.
"Spi maliutka, pochivai	"Sleep, little one, rest,
Glaz svoikh ne otkryvai!"	Do not open your eyes!"

NAHM, NAHM (Egyptian lullaby)

Nahm nahm wa ana ageblak.

Sleep, sleep, and I'll bring you two pairs of pigeons.

◆◆◆

Pat your baby on the bottom, gently and rhythmically, until she falls asleep. This is very commonly sung in Egypt.

FAIS DODO COLIN (French lullaby)

Fais dodo Colin, mon petit frere   Sleep Colin my little brother,
Fais dodo t'aurais du lolo   Sleep, you're going to have sweet milk,
Maman est en haut   Mama is upstairs,
Elle fait des gateaux   Making the cakes,
Pappa est en bas   Pappa is downstairs,
Il fait du chocolat.   Making hot chocolate.

◆◆◆

The French usually rock the baby to sleep with this song,
or pat the baby's bottom rhythmically until the baby
falls asleep.

NUMI NIM (Hebrew lullaby)

Numi numi yeldate
Numi numi nim.
Numi numi kitanti
Numi numi nim.
Abba halach l'avoda
Halach, halach abba
Yashuv eem tset ha levena
Yavi lach matana.

Sleep, sleep, sleep my little child
Sleep, sleep, sleep.
Sleep, sleep, sleep my little one,
Sleep, sleep, sleep.
Your father went to work,
To work your father went,
And with the waning of the moon,
He'll return for you with a present.

CHAPTER 5

Peek-A-Boo

Peek-a-boo play can be seen in many cultures and is, not surprisingly, an important part of an infant's development. You hide your face, then suddenly surprise your baby by where and when you come out. Or, cover baby's face and then let her see you. The greater the surprise, the better, especially as the baby gets older. I had not played peek-a-boo with my four-month-old because it hadn't occurred to me that she would be ready for it. In yet another lesson taught by my four-year-old, however, I found that when the other one would jump from under a table and surprise the baby, the baby loved it. I had never heard so much laughter come from any

baby so small, and needless to say, we started playing peek-a-boo games and songs with her.

The idea of existence and nonexistence, which is the essence of peek-a-boo, is quite significant in linguistic and early child development, as the child gradually becomes aware that what disappears behind a chair will appear again. Notice the delight that early talkers will take in their observations of "all gone apple," or "all gone doggie." Children will tell you this repeatedly; it is fascinating to them.

Remember to vary the peek-a-boo, and try different surprises to delight your baby. She will love the variety.

THERE WERE TWO BLACKBIRDS

There were two blackbirds,	(Both hands behind back)
Sitting on a hill,	
The one named Jack,	(Bring out one hand with index finger up)
The other named Jill.	(Bring out the other hand with index finger up)
Fly away, Jack!	('Fly' hand to behind back)
Fly away, Jill!	('Fly' other hand to behind back)
Come again, Jack!	(Bring back the finger)
Come again, Jill!	(Bring back the other finger)

FRENCH PEEK-A-BOO

Cou cou . . . ah, le voila!

◆◆◆

Hide your face, then look at baby and say, "Here it is!"
(The baby may get frightened if her own face is covered.)

JAPANESE PEEK-A-BOO

Inai, inai,	Nobody's there	(Hands hide face)
Ba-ah-ah.	Boo!	(Take hands away to show face)

PEEK-A-BOO

Peek-a-boo, peek-a-boo,
Who's that hiding there?
Peek-a-boo, peek-a-boo,
Peter's behind the chair.

◆◆◆

This may be played with a baby or by two older children playing together.

HINDI PEEK-A-BOO

Te lol jab!

◆◆◆

The mother takes her sari and covers her face, saying "Te lol." She then shows her face and says "Jah!"

CHAI AAR (Hindi)

Chai aar	Bird comes
Dano kha	Eats some seeds
Pani peene	Drinks a little water
Uri ja!	And flies away!

◆◆◆

Hold the baby's hand, palm up, and "peck" it, making fingers shaped like a beak. Then make your hand "fly" away and disappear behind your back.

•CHAPTER 6•

Feature Plays

Many young babies love to have their faces touched. At about four to six months the baby will be fascinated by your lips, nose, and, in fact, everything about your face. Play these games with your baby when she is too young to touch her face by herself, and when she is older, she will want to try them out on you.

Around this time babies begin to touch and look at their hands, and develop an awareness of where their hands are in space. The coordination of parts of the brain that "see" with those part that "feel" is a big development. Feature games can help in this integration.

KNOCK AT THE DOOR

Knock at the door,   (Pretend to knock on the forehead)

Pull the bell,   (Lightly pull a lock of hair)

Lift the latch,   (Lightly pinch the nose)

And walk in.   (Put your fingers gently on the mouth)

AGARI ME
(Japanese Eye Rhyme)

Agari me
Sagari me
Kuruto ma wa te
Ne ko no me.

Eyes up,
Eyes down,
Round eyes,
Cat's eyes.

TWO LITTLE EYES (Chinese)

Xiao yan-er kan jingzbier,
Xiao bizi wen xiang qi-er,
Xiao erduo ting bao yin-er,
xiao zui-er chi meigui-er.

Two little eyes to look around,	(Touch baby's eyelids or corners of eyes)
Two little ears to hear each sound;	(Touch ears)
One little nose to smell what's sweet,	(Touch nose)
One little mouth that likes to eat.	(Touch lips)

CAT'S EYES

With your finger, make baby's eyes slant at the outside corners, then pull the corners down, then make circles at the corners, and finally cat's eyes. Do this to the baby, but she may enjoy watching you do it to yourself occasionally.

EYE WINKER

Eye winker,   (Point to eyes)
Tom Tinker,   (Point to ears)
Nose smeller,   (Point to nose)
Mouth eater,   (Point to mouth)
Chin chopper,   (Tap chin)
Chin chopper,
Chin chopper,
Chin chopper, chin. (Tickle under chin)

MUSUN-DE
(Japanese Hand Rhyme)

Musun-de,   Make a fist
Hiraite   Open the hand
Te o utte musunde   Clap and make a fist
Mata hiraite,   Open again
Te-o-utte   Clap again
Sono te o ue ni.   Up hands
Sono te o shita ni. Down hands
Sono te o atama ni Touch head
Sono te o me ni.   Touch eyes.

•CHAPTER 7•

Clapping

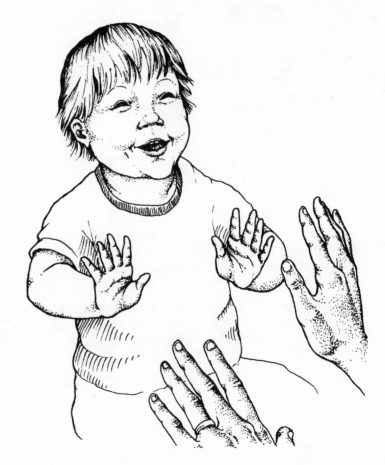

C lapping games will give little babies the giggles and maybe even cause them to burst out laughing. As early as four or five months, babies respond to clapping rhymes, and even though they cannot respond with a clap, they seem to love someone clapping hands on theirs. It creates great delight when an adult takes the hands of a baby and makes a gentle clapping motion. At some time around six months, or a little before, a very important development occurs when a baby can spontaneously bring her hands together in front of her body so that they touch each other. This is the beginning of coordination between the two sides of the body.

PEASE PORRIDGE HOT

Pease porridge hot,
  Pease porridge cold,

Pease porridge in the pot,
  Nine days old.

Some like it hot,
  Some like it cold

Some like it in the pot
  Nine days old.

(Slap hands on knees, then
  together, then clap
  baby's hands twice)

(Alternate clapping hands,
  then clap baby's hands
  and knees)

(Same as above for second
  verse)

PAT-A-CAKE

Pat-a-cake, pat-a-cake,
Baker's man,
Bake me a cake
As fast as you can.
Roll it and pat it,
And mark it with B,
And put it in the oven
For Baby and me.

(Clap your hands—or
  baby's hands)

(Roll baby's hands gently)

CHINESE PAT-A-CAKE

Guang-guang cha,
Guang-guang cha,
  Miao-li heshang
  Mo toufa.

Pat a cake, pat a cake,
Little girl fair,
There's a priest in the temple
Without any hair.

BLINY (Russian "Pat-a-Cake")

Peki bliny rumianye,   Bake pancakes nicely
                     browned,
Rumianye, goriachie.   Nicely browned and hot.
Peki bliny rumianye,   Bake pancakes nicely
                     browned,
Rumianye, goriachie.   Nicely browned and hot.

WARM HANDS

Warm hands, warm—   (Put hands together)
Do you know how?
If you want to   (Rub them)
Warm your hands,
Warm your hands now.

TAPE TAPE PETITES MAINS
(French clapping song)

Tape tape petites mains
Tourne tourne joli moulin
Nous irons dimanche matin
Cueillir les roses du jardin.

Clap, clap little hands	(With your baby on your lap, clap his hands in your hands)
Turn, turn pretty windmill	(Roll baby's hands in your hands towards you)
We are going Sunday morning	(Clap baby's hands to rhythm of the song)
To cut roses from the garden.	

Ta-pe   Ta-pe   pe ti tes mains tour-ne   tour-ne   jo-li mou lin nous fr

-ons di-man-che ma tin cuei uir les ros es du jar-din

WAHAD ETNEN TALATAH
(Egyptian clapping rhyme)

Wahad etnen talatah
Carona Caronatah
Saafuli saafa wa ana
Anot nattah . . . ha, ha!

One, two, three

Carona Caronatah
 [Arabic name]

Clap one clap for me

And I'll jump a jump,
 ha, ha!

(Sing with your baby on your
 lap, clapping to the song)

(At this point, lift your baby
 up for a jump, or if the
 older child is singing, then
 he can jump up and say
 ha, ha!)

POTCHE POTCHE
(Yiddish nursery rhyme, remembered by Sylvia Sucher)

Potche potche kihelach
Mameh vet kafen shichalach
Papa vet kafen zechalach
Und de klayne Kindelach vet
Hubn royte beckalach!

Clap, clap your hands,
Mama will buy you shoes,
Papa will buy you socks,
And the little baby,
Will have such rosy cheeks!

LADUSHKI (Russian Pat-a-Cake)

Ladushki, ladushki!
Gde byli?
-U babushki!
Chto eli?
-Kashku!
Chto pili?
-Brazhku!
Kashka maslianen'ka,
Brazhka sladen'ka,
Babushka dobren'ka.

Ladushki, ladushki!
Where were you?
-At grandmother's!
What did you eat?
-Kasha! (porridge)
What did you drink?
-Brazhka! (home-brew)
The kasha was buttery,
The brazhka was sweet,
The grandmother was kind.

Popili, poeli,

Shu, poleteli!

Na golovku seli!

Seli, posideli,

Proch uleteli!

We drank, we ate,

We fly and we flit (raise baby's hands up high)
We land on the dome (place baby's hands on head)
We sit for a bit,

And off away home! (help baby's hands "fly away")

◆◆◆

Ladushki is an evocative word combining three images, or meanings—clapping hands, chubby little palms, and "precious little one." Clasp the baby's hands rhythmically throughout, until the end of the rhyme when the baby's hands "fly away."

TORTITA, TORTITA
(Panamanian clapping rhyme)

Tortita, tortita,
Tortita de manteca,

(As if making tortita, clap hands three times)

Que lindas manitas
Que tengo yo.

(Turn your hands or baby's hands as if showing off how
pretty they are, moving to the rhythm)

Tortita, tortita,
Tortita made of butter,
Oh, what pretty hands
I have.

TA TA TA LI (Hindi)

Ta ta ta li	Clap your hands
Mamaji ni vali	You are your uncle's favorite
Mamo gaiyo janwar	When your uncle goes out to eat
Bebe gai ramwa.	Baby goes to play.

NAMO GANESHA (Indian chant)

Namo Ganesha,	(Gently clap hands together on "Namo")
Namo Ganesha,	(Gently clap hands together on "Namo")
Namo Ganesha	(Same again, and keep hands together prayer fashion)
Trahimam.	(Bring hands, "prayer fashion," up to face, fingertips touching the nose, and tilt the head down a little when doing so)
Sri Ganesha,	(Hold hands like an open book, palms up, and raise up to the sky, without separating hands)
Sri Ganesha,	(Same again)
Sri Ganesha	(Same again)
Rakshyamam.	(Separate hands and lift to sky, palms up)

Salutation to Ganesha, salutation to Ganesha,
Salutation to Ganesha, the one who guides me [to
   wisdom].

Oh, lucky one, oh, lucky one,
Oh, lucky one, please protect me [from
   ignorance].

◆◆◆

This is an ancient Sanskrit chant, loved by children because the rhyme is so pleasant to say and hear. According
to Hindu scripture, Ganesha is the god of all learning.

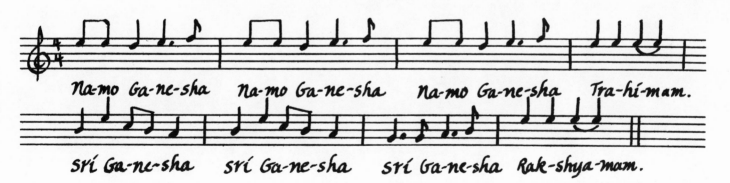

Na-mo Ga-ne-sha   Na-mo Ga-ne-sha   Na-mo Ga-ne-sha   Tra-hí-mam.

Srí Ga-ne-sha   srí Ga-ne-sha   srí Ga-ne-sha   Rak-shya-mam.

•CHAPTER 8•

Bouncing

Bouncing gives great joy to babies and older children. You can bounce the younger ones gently on your knees, and add greater bounces when they begin to seek greater thrills. Bouncing can also be done with the older baby sitting astride the foot: lifting the foot high in the air while you hold the baby's hands. Make the bounces fit in with the rhyme, and include a big bounce somewhere during the "ride."

Slow, soft bouncing seems to pacify restless younger babies, while more vigorous bouncing thrills older ones. The six-month-old baby loves to be moved around, bounced gently, and lifted up. The joy comes from experiencing gravity and movement, which she can now integrate. If the movements are too rough, the baby cannot integrate the sensations—they will disrupt her nervous system and cause her to cry.

TO MARKET, TO MARKET

To market, to market,   (Bounce baby on your
To buy a fat pig;   knees)
Home again, home again,
Jiggety jig.

To market, to market,
To buy a fat hog;
Home again, home again,
Jiggety jog.

TO LONDON TOWN

See-saw, Sacradown,   (Bounce baby on your
Which is the way   knees)
To London Town?
One foot up,
The other down,
That is the way
To London Town.

A FARMER WENT TROTTING

A farmer went trotting upon his grey mare,
Bumpety, bumpety, bump!
With his daughter behind him so rosy and fair,
Lumpety, lumpety, lump!

A magpie cried "Caw," and they all tumbled down,
Bumpety, bumpety, bump!
The mare broke her knees, and the farmer his crown,
Lumpety, lumpety, lump!

The mischevious magpie flew laughing away,
Bumpety, bumpety, bump!
And vowed he would serve them the same the next
  day,
Lumpety, lumpety, lump!

◆◆◆

Hold onto baby while on your lap or knee—this one can
get very bumpy!

EDU-EDU (Russian)

Edu-edu	Here I go
K babe, k dedu,	To Grandmother, to Grandfather
Na loshadke	On a horse
V krasnoi shapke.	Wearing a red hat.
Po rovnoi dorozhke	Along a smooth road
Na odnoi nozhke	With one foot
V starom lapotochke	In an old wooden shoe.
Po rytvinam, po kochkam,	Then along a bumpy road
Vse priamo i priamo,	Straight ahead, straight ahead,
A potom vdrug . . . v iamu!	And then suddenly . . . into a ditch.
BUKH!	BOO!

◆◆◆

Hold baby on your lap and imitate the up-and-down motion of horse riding, at first gently, then more "bumpy." At the "BOO!" you can "drop" the baby between your legs, holding him under the arms.

RIDE A COCK HORSE (English)

Ride a cock horse
To Banbury Cross,
To see a fine lady
Upon a white horse.
With rings on her fingers
And bells on her toes,
She shall have music
Wherever she goes.

(Bounce baby on your knee)

TROT, TROT, TROT

Trot, trot, trot
Go and never stop.
Trudge along my little pony,
Where 'tis rough and where 'tis stony.
Go and never stop,
Trot, trot, trot, trot, trot!

◆◆◆

Use this for a knee ride for a baby, making the bounces
fit in with the rhythm of the rhyme.

HOPPA, HOPPA REITER
(German bouncing rhyme)

Hoppa, hoppa Reiter	Hoppa, hoppa rider,
Wenn er fallt dann schreit er	When he falls down he shouts.
Fallt er in den Graben	When he falls in the ditch,
Fressen ihn die Raben	The ravens will come peck him.
Fallt er in den Sumpf,	When he falls in the mud,
Plumsa!	Plumsa!

◆◆◆

Put your baby or young child on your lap, facing you, and hold his hands while bouncing him. When you say "Plumsa!" hold the baby's hands and let him fall backwards down your legs, and then gently pull him up. For babies under one year, it is better to hold them under the arms.

HAG HOGAGA WA BAT ALLAH
(Egyptian bouncing and lifting song)

Hag Hogaga Wa Bat Allah
Wa Al Kaaba Wa Rasaul Allah
Bedi Asheifak Ya Nabi
Yalli Baladak Baida.

Pilgrim, little pilgrim, house of Allah,
And the Mecca and prophet of Allah,
I am happy to see you, prophet,
Your homeland is very far away.

◆◆◆

Put your child on top of your feet, facing you, and hold her hands. Bounce with a steady, regular beat, as if walking on a pilgrimage.

A PARIS (French)

A Paris, sur un petit cheval gris,	To Paris, on a little grey horse.
A Rouen, sur un petit cheval blanc,	To Rouen, on a little white horse.
Au pas, au pas,	Little steps, little steps.
Au trot, au trot,	Trotting, trotting,
Au galop, au galop!	Galloping, galloping!

◆◆◆

Bounce baby on your lap, making bigger and bigger bounces until the gallop, and then really give her a bounce if she's ready for it.

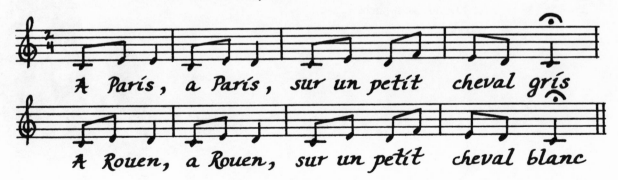

DOCTOR FOSTER
(To the tune of "Yankee Doodle")

Doctor Foster went to
  Gloucester
In a shower of rain,
He stepped in a puddle   (The infant can be
Right up to his middle   "dropped" here.)
And never went there
  again!

ASERRIN, ASERRAN (Spanish)

Aserrin, Aserran	Aserrin, Aserran [saw noise]
Los maderos de San Juan	The woodcutters of San Juan
Piden queso y piden pan	Ask for cheese and ask for bread
Y a los ninos no les dan.	And to the children they give none.

◆◆◆

Cross legs and have baby sit on your feet while holding her hands. Swing the baby, then "drop" on last word of song. A younger baby could be on the lap.

LEG OVER LEG

Leg over leg
As the dog went to Dover.
When he came to a stile,
  Jump, he went over.

(Cross your knees and sit the baby on one ankle, holding his hands. Bounce him to the rhythm of the rhyme, and on "Jump" give him a big swing by uncrossing your knees.)

TROT, TROT TO BOSTON

Trot, trot to Boston,
Trot, trot to Lynn,
Whoops, there's a hole.
Don't fall in!

(Put baby on your lap)

(Baby can be "dropped" between the knees at this point, while holding under the arms)

SAMOAN RHYME

Savalivali means go for a
  walk,

(Hold baby under arms and pretend to walk by gentle bouncing)

Tautalatala means too
  much talk

(Touch baby's mouth)

Alofa ia te oe means I love
  you

(Hug baby)

Take it easy, *faifailemu*.

(Continue to gently rock in hugging position)

A CHEVAL (French)

A cheval, gendarme.	On your horse, policeman.
Les petites dames s'en vont	The little ladies go
Tout-doux, tout-doux, tout-doux,	So softly, so softly, so softly,
Les p'tits messieurs s'en vont	The little gentlemen go
A petits pas, petits pas, petits pas,	Little steps, little steps, little steps,
Les gros paysans s'en vont	The big peasants go
Bordouff, bordouff, bordouff.	Bordouff, bordouff, bordouff.

A Cheval, Gendarme Les petites dames s'en vont tout-doux, tout-doux, tout-doux.....

KINTARO'S RIDE (Japanese)

Masakari katsuida Kintaro	Kintaro carries an ax
Kuma ni matagari ouma no keiko	Practicing horseback riding on a bear.
Haishi do-do hai do-do	Whoa, do-do, whoa, do-do
Haishi do-do hai do-do.	Whoa, do-do, whoa, do-do.

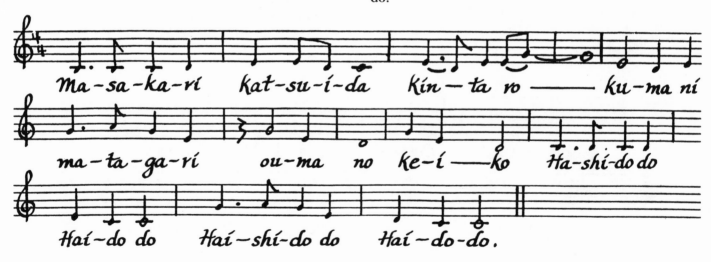

IVORY COAST BOUNCING RHYME

Be be oh sa ton n'gnon dou loo   Don't cry baby. When
                                            your mother comes back,

N'ga mama no e pe nin gome he   She will bring you
she.   something good in her
                                            sack.

◆◆◆

Usually the baby is in a cloth sling on the back of her
mother, who stands and bounces her rhythmically.

DERRY, DOWN DERRY

Derry, down Derry,   (Bounce baby on lap)
   and up in the air,
Baby shall ride
   without pony or mare,
Clasped in my arms   (Hold baby tightly)
   like a queen on a throne,
Prettiest rider   (Continuing to bounce)
   that ever was known.

•CHAPTER 9•

Lifting

Babies will enjoy slow, gentle lifts and drops. These games give the baby a thrill by stimulating those parts of her inner ear which maintain her sense of balance. In turn, this stimulation is also developing her brain. She innately knows what is good for her. Hold the baby firmly so that she feels secure, and make the up and down motion in a way that she likes.

As your baby grows older, she will show signs of wanting more movement, and you can try lifting her higher in the air, even tossing her gently and catching her under the armpits. If you do this, toss her no more than an inch or two, and take care not to hurt her with your thumbs. Waiting until the baby is at least six months old would ensure that her head control is strong enough for such play. Never pull the baby up by the hands—little elbows dislocate easily.

When I sang to my first baby and lifted her high in the air, she wanted to continue the game for ages; I was the one to tire out first. As she grew older, the lifting became higher and higher, and her laughter grew louder. A variation on lifting that she also enjoyed involved lying on my back with my knees bent over my chest. I would put her on my legs and move her around while holding onto her hands.

She particularly liked it when I pretended to make her fall, then stopped my legs just before they reached the floor. The surprise ending was the delight in this game; and it can be incorporated into playing with the nursery rhymes in this chapter.

THE GRAND OLD DUKE OF YORK

The grand old Duke of York	
He had ten thousand men.	
He marched them up to the top of the hill	(Lift baby)
And he marched them down again.	(Lower baby)
And when they were up, they were up,	(Lift again)
And when they were down, they were down,	(Lower again)
And when they were only halfway up	(Lift halfway)
They were neither up nor down.	(Lift up and lower)

JACK-IN-THE-BOX

Jack-in-the-box,   (Sit baby on lap)
   all shut up tight,
Not a breath of air
   or a ray of light,
How tired he must be,
   all folded up.
Let's open the lid,
   and up he'll jump!   (Lift baby high in the air)

MIX A PANCAKE

Mix a pancake,   (Hold baby and help her
Stir a pancake,   make big stirring motions)
Pop it in the pan.   ("Pop" baby down onto lap)

Fry the pancake,   (Rock her gently from side to side)
Toss the pancake,   (Lift her high . . .
Catch it if you can! and bring her down)

ZAIKA BELEN'KII SIDIT (Russian)

Zaika belen'kii sidit,	Little white rabbit sits
On ushami shevelit.	Wiggling his ears. (Wiggle baby's ears)
Vot tak, vot tak	This way and that
On ushami shevelit.	He wiggles his ears.
Zaike knolodno sidet',	Little rabbit is cold (Clap baby's hands)
Nado lapochki pogret',	And must warm his paws,
Khlop, khlop, khlop, khlop,	Clap, clap, clap, clap,
Nado lapochki pogret'.	And must warm his paws.
Zaike kholodno stoiat',	Little rabbit is cold standing up.
Nado zaike poskakat',	He must hop. (Lift, in hopping motion)
Skok-skok, skok-skok,	Hop-hop, hop-hop,
Nado zaike poskakat'.	He must hop.
Kto-to zaiku ispugal,	Someone frightened the little rabbit.
Zaichik pryg . . . i ubezhal.	He jumped up . . . and ran away. (Lift high into the air)

UNDER THE WATER

Under the water, under the sea,
Catching fishes for my tea.
Dead or alive?

◆◆◆

Hold baby horizontally, looking at her as you bend over and chant the above. Afterwards you can say happily, "Alive!" and lift her up. When child grows old enough to talk, she has the choice of answering "dead" or "alive." If she says "dead," you "drop" her on the floor, making the drop gentle or scary depending on her age and sensitivity. If she says "alive," lift her high in the air and then stand her on her feet.

POP GOES THE WEASEL

All around the carpenter's
   bench
The monkey chased the weasel.
The monkey thought it was all
   in fun,
Pop goes the weasel!

◆◆◆

(Lift the baby at "Pop,"
   and make it as high
   as baby likes)

TATAH HABAH HABAH
(Egyptian walking rhyme)

Tatah Habah Habah
Tatah Khati El Atabah.

Tatah, step by step
Tatah, one foot into the threshold.

◆◆◆

In Egypt, when a baby is first learning to walk, an adult will take his hands and hold him up while he moves his feet in a walking fashion.

HA KE YOI
(Japanese wrestling rhyme)

Ha ke yoi	Get ready,
No ko ta	Go!

◆◆◆

This is what the huge sumo wrestlers say before a wrestle. Japanese parents like to play this with their children when they are learning how to stand. Hold onto the baby's hands and jiggle the arms, or lift the baby high from under the armpits.

THISTLE-SEED (Chinese)

Lao gua piao, lao gua piao,
Hunshen shangxia chang bai mao,
Chen zhuo feng-er chuishanggu,
Diao zai di-shang shuaibuzhao.

Thistle-seed, thistle-seed,   (Hold baby and rock,
Fly away, fly.   sway from side to side)

The hair on your body   (Lift baby high)
Will take you up high.

Let the wind whirl you   (Hold baby and twirl
Around and around.   around)

You'll not hurt yourself
When you fall to the ground.   ("Drop" baby gently to the
                                                    ground or bed, but don't
                                                    let go of her!)

SEE-SAW

See-saw, Marjorie-Daw,
Jackie shall have a new
   master.
He can't earn but a penny
   a day,
Because he can't work any
   faster.

(Bounce baby on your foot
   to the rhythm)

PULLING THE SAW (Chinese)

La da ju.
Che da ju.
Yong da tou gai fangzi.
Gei beibei qu niangzi.

We push the big saw,
We push the big saw,
To saw up the wood
To build us a house
In order that baby
May have a good spouse.

◆◆◆

This can be played in two ways. One is to sit the baby on your foot, and, holding her hands, rock her gently backwards and forwards. Another version can be played when she is old enough to sit up. Sitting her in front of you on the floor, do a gentle "push-me-pull-you" motion, so that you both stretch forward a bit, then backward, in a sawing motion.

•CHAPTER 10•

Tickling

Tickling is probably the first type of play that the baby experiences, when she is lightly tickled by visitors on the cheeks or on the toes. There are many forms of tickling, and experimentation with your baby will let you know what she likes and where she likes it. Most babies differ slightly in their responses and desires, and some differ greatly. Tickling requires careful awareness by the parent, as the fragile line between fun and feeling trapped can be crossed in a matter of seconds, making the infant uncomfortable and unhappy. When tickling is light, intermittent, and short, it is usually the most effective.

Tickling requires complete respect for your baby. It is an invasion of her being, in a sense, and can be disruptive if done insensitively. Observe your baby carefully for any sign that she does not seem to be enjoying the tickle.

Tickling can be done with fingers, hair, soft pieces of material, or with your lips. The different sensations are appreciated by babies, and variation increases the enjoyment. Kiss-tickles on bare skin, blowing or making guppy-like movements with your mouth also cause tickling sensations.

Sometimes, when the baby or child is not in the mood for an all-out laugh session, a light tickle is perfect for relaxing and pleasing the baby in a more gentle way. As soon as my daughter responded to tickling, at around four months or so, my husband began to give her "tickle massages" when she needed quieting, or before sleep. This is his specialty, and I have never quite been able to duplicate his tickle massage to her satisfaction. Even now, at the age of four years, she will frequently ask for a tickle massage at bedtime, and she smiles and drifts quickly into sleep. He will run his fingers very lightly over her body, concentrating on the area of her back and legs, in light circles. If he strays to her sides, she will tense up because he has moved into a more sensitive tickling area, and before sleep she prefers the light touch, even after a slightly more vigorous tickle session.

A light tickle is similarly used in traditional Japanese homes to relax the infant or older children before bedtime. Like an adult's massage, the stretching of the body and the limbs of the baby during a good tickle will usually relax the baby enormously, or, in other terms, clear the energy channels, allowing a deep sleep to come more easily. Care must be taken here to keep the tickle light, or else you might stimulate your baby into an alert state, ready for more play.

Tickling with the nursery rhymes in this section can be great fun, and your child might eventually try them out on you. You can vary their rhythms, or try adding a surprise by holding your hand high in the air before the descent into the tickle at the end.

THIS LITTLE PIG

This little piggie went to market,
This little piggie stayed home;
This little piggie had roast beef,
This little piggie had none.
This little piggie cried, "Wee-wee-wee,
I can't find my way home."

(Hold each toe in turn, starting with the big one, and on
the last line tickle underneath the baby's foot, or in
another ticklish spot.)

OLD CHANG THE CRAB (Chinese)

Lao Zhang, Lao Zhang,
Tou-ding po-kuang
Jianzi liang-ba
Kuaizi si-shuang.

Old man Chang,   (Move one hand like a crab)
I've often heard it said,
You wear a basket upon   (Put the other hand flat on
  your head;   the crab)
You've two pairs of scissors   (Move two fingers like
  to cut up your meat,   scissors)
And two pairs of chopsticks   (Tickle baby with thumb
with which you eat.   and index finger like
                                           chopsticks)

SHOE A LITTLE HORSE

Shoe a little horse,
Shoe a little mare,
But let the little colt
Go bare, bare, bare.

◆◆◆

(Say this rhyme while patting the baby's feet)

SOROKA (Russian)

Soroka-beloboka	White feathered magpie
Kashku varila.	Boiled porridge
Detok kormila.	To feed her children.
Etomu dala,	She gave it to this one,
Etomu dala,	And to this one,
Etomu dala,	And to this one,
Etomu dala,	And to this one,
A etomu ne dala.	And to this one she gave none.
Ty vodu ne nosil,	You did not bring water,
Drov ne rubil,	You did not chop wood,
Kashi ne varil,	You did not boil porridge,
Tebe net nichego.	You get nothing.

◆◆◆

Take the baby's hand, palm up, and with your index finger make circular, "stirring" movements on the palm. Then bend the fingers, one by one, except the thumb. When you say, "You did not . . . ," take baby's thumb and rotate it gently.

Another version:

Tut pen',	Here's a stump,
Tut koloda,	Here's a log,
Tut kipiatok, kipiatok.	Here's boiling hot water.

◆◆◆

Touch the baby's wrists, then inside the elbow, and then tickle the arm.

BABY BYE

Baby bye, here's a fly	(Walk your fingers on
We must watch him	baby's face)
You and I.	
There he goes,	
On his toes,	
Over baby's nose.	

SLOWLY, SLOWLY

Slowly, slowly, very slowly   (Use your fingers to
Creeps the garden snail.   "creep" on the baby)

Slowly, slowly, very slowly
Up the wooden rail.

Quickly, quickly, very quickly (Change tempo)
Runs the little mouse.
Quickly, quickly, very quickly
Round about the house.

CATERPILLAR

"Who's that tickling my back?" (Crawl your fingers
   said the wall.   across your baby's
"Me," said a small caterpillar,   tickle spots)
"I'm learning to crawl."

SNAIL SONG

The snail is so slow, the snail   (Creep along the
   is so slow,   arms, legs, or
He creeps and creeps along.   any ticklish
And as he does he sings his song: place)
The snail is so-o-o s-l-o-w.

ADI EL BADAH
(Egyptian tickling rhyme)

Adi el badah,
Wa adi elly ashtaraha
Wa adi elly salaaha
Wa adi elly asharha
Wa adi elly ahl haty
Hetta hetta hetta!

Here is the egg,   (Take your baby's hand,
                 and fold the little finger down)

Who bought it   (Fold the ring finger down)
And who boiled it   (Fold the middle finger down)
And who peeled it   (Fold the index finger down)
And who said give me a   (Fold the thumb, and then
Piece, piece, piece!   tickle under baby's arm)

PETIT POUCE
(French tickling rhyme)

Toc, toc, toc
Petit pouce, lève-toi!
Chut, je dors . . .
Hop! Je sors!
Et je vais chatouiller
Ton petit ventre!

Knock, knock, knock (Knock on a table three times)

Little thumb, get up. (Put your hand in a fist and raise thumb)

Shhh, I'm sleeping. ("Shhh" with finger to lips, and put hands together by your ear for "sleep")

Hop! I pop up! (Pop your thumb up,

And I will tickle   and tickle your baby's stomach)

Your little stomach!

PAO PAO PAO (Ivory Coast)

Pao Pao Pao (Gently pat palm of baby's hand three times)

Caca bi ni ni ni ni. (Pretend to be a little crawling ant and "crawl" up baby's arm, tickling lightly)

KAI KURI
(Japanese hand game)

Kai kuri   To haul in a rope, hand over hand

Kai kuri
To to no me.   Fish eye

◆◆◆

This game is many centuries old, and has taken on some regional differences over the years. Often it is played like this: hold baby's hands and roll them around each other, towards the baby. At "*to to no me*," gently tap the baby's elbows together.

ROUND THE GARDEN

Round and round the
   garden
Went the Teddy Bear,
  One step,
  Two steps,
Tickly under there.

(Run your index finger
   round the baby's palm)

("Jump" your finger up
   his arm)
(Tickle him under his arm)

Round and round the
   haystack,
Went the little mouse,
  One step,
  Two steps,
In his little house.

(Repeat the same actions
   for the second verse)

THIS LITTLE COW EATS GRASS

This little cow eats grass,
This little cow eats hay;
This little cow drinks water;
This little cow runs away;
This little cow does nothing
But just lies down all day.
We'll chase her,
We'll chase her,
We'll chase her away!

Point to each finger in turn, starting with the thumb;
tickle the little finger and then up the baby's arm.

LITTLE MOUSIE

See the little mousie   (Touch index and middle
                              fingers to thumb for
                              "mouse")

Creeping up the stair   (Creep mouse slowly up
                              other forearm, bent at
                              elbow)

Looking for a warm nest.

There—Oh! There.   (Let mouse spring into
                              elbow corner—tickle)

AY MAMA (Spanish)

Ay mama, abi viene Vicente;	Ay mama, here comes Vicente;
Sacale la silla para que se siente,	Pull up a chair for him,
Y si no se sienta,	And if he doesn't sit down,
Mandelo a la plaza	Send him to the plaza
A vender mostaza,	To sell mustard,
Y si no la vende,	And if he doesn't sell it,
Puyele la panza!	Punch him in the tummy!

◆◆◆

Clap hands with baby, alternating hands, and tickle baby
at the end with a mock "punch."

UNE POULE SUR UN MUR (French)

Une poule sur un mur
Qui picotati du pain dur
Picoti picota
Leve la queue
Et saute en bas!

A hen sits on a wall,   (Sit baby on your lap and
Pecking at hard bread.   "peck" bread in his hand)
Picoti picota   (Continue to peck to
Raises her tail,   rhythm of verse)
And jumps below!   (Hand "jumps" and tickles
                                    baby's feet)

•CHAPTER 11•

Finger Play

Finger plays are good for even the youngest of babies, who grow more and more interested as they begin to manipulate their own fingers. Finger plays were far more popular earlier in this century and played a greater role in the child's language development. Children don't grow tired of these rhymes and finger movements for years; my four-year-old still begs me to sing them to her.

LITTLE BIRD

I saw a little bird
  go hop, hop, hop.

(Rest index and tall
  fingers on baby's
  thumb; make bobbing
  motion from wrist)

I told the little bird
  to stop, stop, stop.

(Point each "stop" with
  index finger)

I went to the window
  to say, "How do you do?"

(Extend hand as if to
  shake hands)

He wagged his little tail,

(Rest index and tall
  fingers on thumb; curl
  other index finger and
  attach at back of hand
  like a tail)

And away he flew.

(Fly fingers over head
  and behind back)

1, 2, 3

1, 2, 3

(Rest three fingertips on
  your baby's palm)

Father caught a flea

("Pick" a flea off your
  baby's palm)

Put him in the teapot

(Close your baby's hand by
  curling her fingers)

To drink a cup of tea.

(Bring imaginary teacup—
  your baby's hand—to
  your mouth and kiss it)

THIS LITTLE DOGGIE

This little doggie ran away to
  play,

This little doggie said, "I'll go
  too someday."
This little doggie began to dig
  and dig,
This little doggie danced a
  funny jig.
This little doggie cried, "Ki! Yi!
  Ki! Yi!
I wish I were big."

◆◆◆

Hold up fingers of one hand
and point to each finger in turn.

ULU, UAUAU
(Samoan touching rhyme)

Ulu, uauau, tulivae tamatamivae
Tulivae tamatamaivae, tulivae tamatamaivae
Ulu, uauau tulivae tamatamaivae
Mata, taliga, gutu male isu.

Head, shoulders, knees and
    toes,
Knees and toes, knees and
    toes,
Head, shoulders, knees and
    toes,
Eyes, ears, mouth and nose.

(Hold baby's hand and
touch the appropriate
parts of his body)

FAMILY FINGERS

This is the father, short
  and stout,
This is the mother with
  children all about.
This is the brother, tall
  you see,
This is the sister with
  dolly on her knee.
This is the baby, sure to
  grow,
And here is the family,
  all in a row.

(Point to each finger in
turn, starting with the
thumb)

(Gently grab baby's whole
hand)

HERE IS A HOUSE

Here is a house built up high,	(Stretch arms up, touching fingertips like a roof)
With two tall chimneys reaching the sky.	(Stretch arms up separately)
Here are the windows,	(Make square shape with hands)
Here is the door.	(Knock)
If we peep inside, we'll see a mouse on the floor.	(Raise hands in fright)

FIVE FINGERS

Five fingers on this hand,	(Hold up one hand)
Five fingers on that;	(Hold up the other hand)
A sweet little nose,	(Point to nose)
A mouth like a rose,	(Point to mouth)
Two cheeks so tiny and fat.	(Point to each cheek)
Two eyes, two ears,	(Point to each)
And ten little toes;	(Point to toes)
That's the way the baby grows.	

PAL'CHIK-MAL'CHIK (Russian)

Pal'chik-mal'chik	Little boy-finger
Gde ty byl?	Where have you been?
S etim bratsem	With this little brother
V les khodil.	I went to the woods.
S etim bratsem	With this little brother
Shchi varil.	I made soup.
S etim bratsem	With this little brother
Kashu el.	I ate porridge.
S etim bratsem	With this little brother
Pasni pel.	I sang a song.

◆◆◆

Holding baby's thumb, bend remaining fingers down, one after another.

FRÈRE JACQUES
(French hand game)

Frère Jacques, Frère Jacques,
Dormez-vous? Dormez-vous?
Sonnez les matines! Sonnez les matines!
Din, dan, don. Din, dan, don.

Are you sleeping,   (Place hands together by
  are you sleeping,   ear and close eyes)
Brother John,
Brother John?
Morning bells are ringing, (Alternate hands in pulling
Morning bells are ringing,   bell ropes)
Din, dan, don,   (Continue pulling ropes)
  din, dan, don.

◆◆◆

Although this rhyme is heard time and time again, children never seem to tire of it.

frè-re Jac-ques, frè-re Jac-ques! Dor-mez-vous? Dor-mez-vous. Son-nez les ma-

ti-nes! Son-nez les ma-ti-nes! Din, dan, don, din, dan, don!

WHERE IS THUMBKIN?
(To tune of "Frere Jacques")

Where is Thumbkin?   (Put hands behind back)
Where is Thumbkin?
Here I am. Here I am.   (Show one thumb, then the
                               other)

How are you this   (Bend one thumb)
  morning?
Very well, I thank you.   (Bend other thumb)
Run and play. Run and   (Put hands behind back)
  play.

Where is Pointer?
Where is Pointer?
Here I am. Here I am.   (Show one index finger,
                               then the other)

How are you this   (Bend one index finger)
  morning?
Very well, I thank you.   (Bend other index finger)
Run and play. Run and   (Put hands behind back)
  play.

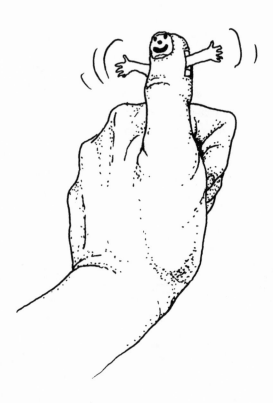

Where is Tall Man?
Where is Tall Man?
Here I am. Here I am.   (Show one tall finger, then
                                the other)

How are you this   (Bend one tall finger)
    morning?
Very well, I thank you.   (Bend other tall finger)
Run and play. Run and   (Put tall fingers behind
    play.   back)

Where is Feeble Man?
Where is Feeble Man?
Here I am. Here I am.   (Show one ring finger, then
                                the other)

How are you this   (Bend one ring finger)
    morning?
Very well, I thank you.   (Bend other ring finger)
Run and play. Run and   (Put ring fingers behind
    play.   back)

Where is Baby?
Where is Baby?
Here I am. Here I am.   (Show one baby finger,
                                then the other)

How are you this   (Bend one baby finger)
    morning?
Very well, I thank you.   (Bend other baby finger)
Run and play. Run and   (Put baby fingers behind
    play.   back)

Where are all the Men?
Where are all the Men?
Here we are. Here we are. (Show all fingers on one
                               hand, then the other)

How are you this   (Bend fingers of one hand)
    morning?
Very well, we thank you.   (Bend fingers of other hand)
Run and play. Run and   (Put hands behind back)
    play.

LES PETITES MARIONNETTES (French)

Ainsi font font font
Les petites marionnettes,
Ainsi font font font
Les petites marionnettes.

Trois petits tours
Marionnettes marionnettes
Trois petits tours
Et puis s'en vont!

Ain-sí font font font   les pe-tí-tes mar-ío-net-tes, aín-sí

font font font   les pe-tí-tes   mar-ío-net-tes

Move like this this this   (Hold baby's hands up
                               and twist front and
                               back at wrist)

Little puppets, little puppets,
Move like this this this
Oh, the little puppets do.

Three little turns,   (Make three twists of
                              hands, as for above
                              verse)

Little puppets, little puppets,
Take three little turns,
And then they go away!   (Hands fly away behind
                              back)

◆◆◆

When baby is old enough, he will be able to imitate your
movements to this rhyme by himself.

HERE'S A BALL FOR BABY

Here's a ball for baby,
Big and soft and round.

(Put the baby's hands
   together to make a ball,
   fingertips touching)

Here is baby's hammer,
Oh, how he can pound!

(Hands in fists, pounding
   one on top of the other)

Here is baby's music,
Clapping, clapping so.

(Clap hands)

Here are baby's soldiers,
Standing in a row.

(Hold hands up, fingers
   outstretched)

Here is baby's trumpet,
Toot-too-too, too-too.
Here's the way that baby
Plays at "Peek-a-boo."

(Bring fists to mouth, like a
   trumpet)
(Fingers partially cover
   eyes)

Here's a big umbrella,
Keeping baby dry.
Here is the baby's cradle
Rock-a-baby-bye.

(Put palm flat over pointed
   finger of bottom hand)
(Interlace fingers, with
   index fingers pointing up
   and touching, and rock
   the "cradle")

POINT TO THE RIGHT

Point to the right of me,
Point to the left of me,
Point up above me,
Point down below.
Right, left, up,
And down so slow.

(Use both arms and follow
   action slowly)

(Increase speed in pointing)
(Decrease speed)

References

Association for Childhood Education International, *Sung Under the Silver Umbrella*. New York: Macmillan & Co., 1935.

Ayres, A. Jean. *Sensory Integration and the Child*. Los Angeles: Western Psychological Services, 1979.

Center for Sensory Integration International, 1402 Grovens Ave., Torrance, CA 90501

Colbin, Annemarie. *The Book of Whole Meals*. New York: Random House, Inc., 1983.

————. *Food and Healing*. New York: Random House, Inc., 1986.

Grayson, Marion. *Let's Do Fingerplays*. Washington: Robert B. Luce, Inc., 1962.

Kavanaugh, Michelle. "What Makes Babies Cry?" *Mother's Manual* (March–April 1976): 32–34.

Klaus, M.H., and J.H. Kennel. *Maternal Infant Bonding*. St. Louis: C.V. Mosby Company, 1976.

Liedloff, Jean. *The Continuum Concept*. New York: Warner Books, 1977.

Matterson, Elizabeth, comp. *Games for the Young: Fingerplays and Nursery Games*, New York: The American Heritage Press, 1971.

McCarty, Meredith. *American Macrobiotic Cuisine*. Eureka, CA: Turning Point Publications, 1986.

McDougall, John A., M.D., and Mary A. Mc Dougall. *The McDougall Plan*. Piscataway, NJ: New Century Publishers, Inc., 1983.

Miller, Saul, and Jo Anne Miller. *Food for Thought: A New Look at Food And Behavior*. Englewood Cliffs, NJ: Prentice-Hall, Inc. 1979.

Montagu, Ashley. *Touching: The Human Significance of the Skin*. New York: Harper & Row, 1978.

Pearce, Joseph Chilton, *Magical Child*. New York: E.P. Dutton Co., 1977.

Peiper, Albrecht. "Cerebral Function in Infancy and Childhood," New York: Consultants Bureau, 1963.

Poulsson, Emilie. *Finger Plays for Nursery and Kindergarten*. New York: Dover Publications, 1971.

Reed, Barbara. *Food, Teens and Behavior*. Manitowoc, WI: Natural Press, 1983. (Can be ordered from the publisher at PO Box 2107, Manitowoc, WI 54220.)

Restak, Richard M. *The Brain: The Last Frontier*. New York: Doubleday & Co., 1979.

Rice, Ruth D. "Premature Infants Respond to Sensory Stimulation." *American Psychiatric Association Monitor* (November 1975).

Samuels, M., and N. Samuels. *The Well Baby Book*. New York: Simon & Shuster, Inc., 1979.

Schauss, Alexander G. *Diet, Crime and Delinquency*. Berkeley, CA: Parker House, 1981.

Schneider, Vimala. *Infant Massage*. New York: Bantam Books, Inc., 1979.

Dr. Seuss. *One Fish, Two Fish, Red Fish, Blue Fish*. New York: Random House, Inc., 1960.

Sobel, Laura. Interview with author. Santa Barbara, CA, March, 1983. Address: P.O. Box 884, Summerland, CA. 93067.

Stevenson, Burton Egbert, comp. *The Home Book of Verse for Young Folks*. New York: Holt, Rinehart & Winston, 1929.

Tara, William. *Better Health Through Nutrition*. London: Community Health Foundation, 1977.

Thevenin, Tine. *The Family Bed*. 1976. (Available through author at Avery Publishers, 350 Thornes Ave., Garden City Park, NY 11040

United States Senate, Select Committee on Nutrition and Human Needs. *Dietary Goals for the United States*. Washington, D.C., 1977.

Vezie, Mary B. "Sensory Integration: A Foundation for Learning." *Academic Therapy* 10 (Spring 1975): 345–54.